Welcome to this visual and conceptual practice of living in the questions. I have created these tools to guide you through the idea of questioning. This is a part of a visioning and manifesting practice.

Having our hopes and desires come true is just a small part of what takes place when we live in the questions. This is a practice of clearing and, we hope, of healing. All the things that are blocking you from "you" can be uncovered, discovered and removed.

The ideas that are denying you your true greatness, your gifts and your purpose can be resolved and cleared. You are a living vibration in a human body; you have awareness. You are already awakened. Now that you have arrived here, let's explore the idea of your wholeness and tune into your place in this world. To do this, it helps to have a wider perspective and see things with an open mind and heart. Living in the unknown can be a very courageous act fraught with fear and uncertainty; most of us choose what we know. It feels cozy and familiar. But if we don't open up, we won't grow, we can't expand. Most of us want to live a life of joy, peace and success. We want to leave a legacy that has a positive impact on the world and those around us. If this is you, then welcome to the questions. Welcome to the unknowingness of life.

If you are a seeker, then finding the answers is your mission. "How can I do this?" "What can I do to get here or there?" "Why is this happening right now?" "How elevated can I get?" Finding the answers is an interesting construct that we see explorers and scientists embark upon every day. We are humans; we want to get in there and meddle with things, accomplish goals, reach for the stars and navigate exactly how that looks.

We concoct all sorts of ways to make change and impact our world so that we can feel loved, safe and successful. Most of us strive and dig deep to support our ideas and dreams so we can make a better life for our families and loved ones. Many of us want so badly to change the world and make our mark ... you name it. We, as humans, are "doing it." As long as we are in the "doing" we don't have to live in the dreaded mystery of not knowing. Get a degree, find a great job, stay the course, save for retirement, invest in this stock, walk across that stage... On and on. That is the doing and the seeking of the answers. It can be exhausting. This practice gives you permission to take an action and then let go of the outcome.

# Manifesting

You may have heard a lot about the law of attraction - the ability to attract into our lives whatever we are focusing on - it is a very popular practice that has gotten a lot of traction over the years.

The Law of Attraction practice is a powerful tool many embrace, however the truth is that most of the time we are short-changing ourselves. Often, we simply base our reflections through the lens of our life experience, on the goals and ideas that society, family and teachers have imposed upon us. These influences may have served us well for many years, but it is important not to allow them to block the universe from uncovering exactly what is meant for our highest purpose and vibration.

Perhaps you feel stressed, or the world is pushing down on a certain area of your life. Maybe you feel pressure over money, your career or family. Maybe you are uncertain in your spiritual quest and just seek guidance and motivation.

Sometimes the methods we seek to help us cope with these stresses just compound the issue. Instead of seeking the answer to "Why is this the way it is?" or "What is wrong here?" We try to ask questions that empower us – the universe will always answer.

Quiet, focused meditation can be a wonderful way to open yourself up to the possibilities of the universe. But for some people meditation is a difficult practice; that is why I have created these tools. I hope that this card deck and workbook will become key instruments for envisioning your success and developing your practice.

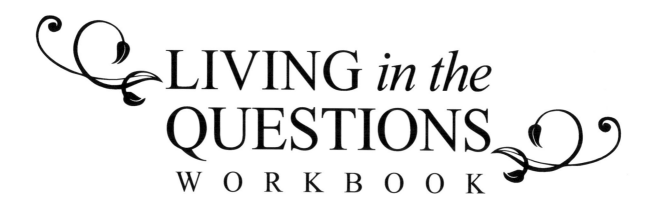

# LIVING *in the* QUESTIONS
## WORKBOOK

*This work is dedicated to my tribe.*

*This is for all of you who carry me through the "Why's" and the "WTF's."*

*This is for my tribe, from the street to the temple, from the bedroom to the backyard.*

*This is for every question already answered and for every mystery that is the gift of the unknown.*

*To my spirit animals: the streets dogs of the planet and my baby raven, Peanut, who fell from the tree.*

*Life is in session. Keep Living in the Questions, family. We got this…*

*Thank you.*
*Love, David*

# Listening

This exercise is created to empower you and prepare you to ask questions that open you up to seeing the answers in front of you. This is a tool that helps you move into a space of allowing. Make no mistake about it - this is not a random act of blind faith. You do not just wait for the universe to deliver. Your actions count, and there is real-life value in taking small consistent actions and getting lasting results. The energy and frequency you express are based on inward sincerity and presence. (That is the fancy talk for "what you put into this you get out of it" so be sure to set your intentions). Get quiet and focus from time to time. Getting into the present moment throughout the day will help a great deal, and reflecting on the exercises will often get you there.

I have this great practice that I do almost daily. I visualize myself placing my ear against a wall and trying to hear what's on the other side. In my short meditation, I can see myself in silence trying to be as quiet as possible. My ear is on the veil of the world; I am in the moment. I just listen deeply and peacefully. In that brief silence there are no answers, no ideas, just nothingness. You can do this at the checkout stand - let a couple of people get in front of you and take a moment to place your ear on the invisible wall and listen deeply. See your chest sink into your breath and move your awareness into the moment. Reflect on your question with wonder and curiosity and then let it go.

What I have learned is that we don't just listen with our ears or insight. We also listen with our vision and our actions; we walk toward what is pulling us, what is calling to us. We see coincidences and aligning events happening around us and things sync up.

It takes practice, but soon we become in tune with the vibration of our questions and we begin to realize the universe is always answering. It answers in actionable life events. Sometimes, unexpectedly, we will experience a very welcome change taking place. Surprises and good news seem to cascade in our lives as we take our hands off the wheel and let life drive for a while. Of course things will change, they always do.

Do not be discouraged when contrast takes place. You may feel the shake up of your daily life. Things may even appear to be falling apart or becoming chaotic. This is normal; that is the universe at work. That is the dance of life as we know it. Let the movement begin and allow things to just happen. Be present; let go of things you are trying to control. Soon, and sometimes very quickly, your life will launch into the place you have been working toward for a long time. So keep coming back to the exercise and practice "Living in the Questions."

We don't always need the answers. With a little patience you will find that the universe has been conspiring all along to grant you much more than you could have ever imagined.

The time has come to take your true place in the world, living and doing what you love, what you are compelled to do, what you came here to do.

The universe is answering. Are you listening?

*David P. Wichman*

# Welcome to the "Living in the Questions"
 ## Journal/Workbook

## This is the companion book for the LITQ card deck

**Why :**

Austrian poet Rainer Maria Rilke once wrote: "Have patience with everything unresolved in your heart and try to love the questions themselves as if they were locked rooms or books written in a very foreign language… Live the questions now. Perhaps then, someday far in the future, you will gradually, without even noticing it, live your way into the answer."

This practice is all about embracing those questions without always trying to rush straight to the answers. This is the practice of allowing, of letting things come to you and unlocking that powerful tool that is your higher awareness.

### Why 72 days!

(The 21 days to a new habit myth)

**The science:**

This is a 72 day practice that helps you develop the habit of seeing the world you live in from a different perspective.

Sometimes in life we hear certain beliefs and theories repeated so often that they almost become fact. One of those is the idea that it takes 21 days to create a new habit. It is often referenced in books or on transformative television shows, but where did the idea actually come from?

James Clear, author of the bestselling book *Atomic Habits*, investigated the origins of the belief that it takes 21 days to form new habits and discovered a fascinating answer. The term was reportedly coined by plastic surgeon Maxwell Maltz in the 1950s based on his own experiences trying to change his behaviors.

Maltz later included the idea in his 1960 book *Psycho-Cybernetics*, stating: "These, and many other commonly observed phenomena tend to show that it requires a minimum of about 21 days for an old mental image to dissolve and a new one to jell." The book went on to become a blockbuster and sold more than 30 million copies.

James Clear explains: "In the decades that followed, Maltz's work influenced nearly every major 'self-help' professional from Zig Ziglar to Brian Tracy to Tony Robbins. And as more people recited Maltz's story — like a very long game of 'telephone' — people began to forget that he said 'a minimum of about 21 days' and shortened it to, 'it takes 21 days to form a new habit.'"

And so the myth about forming new habits in 21 days was born.

———

Recent research has revealed that the reality is much different. A University College London study published in the *European Journal of Social Psychology* was led by health psychology researcher Phillippa Lally and examined the habits of 96 people over a 12-week period. The study found it actually takes more than two months to form a new habit. In fact, the exact findings showed it can take anywhere from 18 to 254 days to form a new habit, pinpointing the key figure at 66 days.

There is a huge variation in those figures, which is why I have designed this workbook for 72 days, allowing you that extended period to form the habit of living in the questions, instead of constantly seeking answers, as so often happens in our instant gratification society.

The simple daily practice takes about two minutes, and within 72 days you will see changes happening all around you. You can use this workbook as a journal for as long as you like. I imagine that very quickly most of you will create empowering questions of your own even forgoing the card deck after a while. I do hope you will share them with me. What an exciting adventure we are on.

So let's get started...

# The Practice:

Keep the workbook and card deck next to your bed or in a sitting area. Each morning and evening, when you wake and before you go to sleep, do the simple exercises on each page. Remember, this is a practice. If you miss a day or two it is perfectly fine. Even doing this once a week works great.

## How:

Take a few moments to center yourself and reflect on something that brings you great joy. Focus on that feeling for a moment. It may be a person, perhaps even a pet or a fantastic fantasy that you love to daydream about. Or seeing a baby filled with wonder. Imagine that joy and excitement. Embody that feeling while shuffling or mixing the cards. Putting positive energy into your intentional shuffling sets the tone for the day.

Each card in the deck presents you a question to envision.

When pulling a card try not to seek the answers. Just observe the thoughts about what is possible. Use your imagination, and if the card you pull doesn't resonate with you then pull another. There is no right or wrong here.

Leave the seeking to the universe. This is a practice of allowing and listening. Try becoming the observer in your life. Find yourself being present for what is happening around you. Let go of the judgment or desire to control. Let the synchronicity you encounter guide you. Sometimes things that look like they are falling apart are actually falling together. That is the universe moving things out of the way.

Remember: Be patient with yourself. Enjoy the process and have fun.

## Morning

*Each morning after you draw a card, using the Living in the Questions workbook/journal, record your practice.*

**1:** Write one thing that you are grateful for, something that brings you great joy. — JOSH

**2:** Write out the question you drew from the deck. — WHO WOULD I BE WYONT THIS THOUGHT HOLDING ME BACK

**3:** Write one action you are willing to take today that moves you toward the question. — GO TO GYM, RESIST THE TIRED

**4:** Do a short meditation of 1-2 minutes, just focusing on what's possible.

## Evening

*At night use the workbook or a journal to write about your day.*

**1:** Write one thing you did that brought you joy today.

**2:** Write one thing you did that you would like to do better tomorrow.

**3:** Then write one thing you will commit to do tomorrow that brings joy.

*If you experienced an answer to a question you drew, journal about it.*

**"Soon you will see that the universe has been conspiring all along to grant you much more than you could ever imagine."**

**— DP Wichman**

So make sure you keep living in the questions.

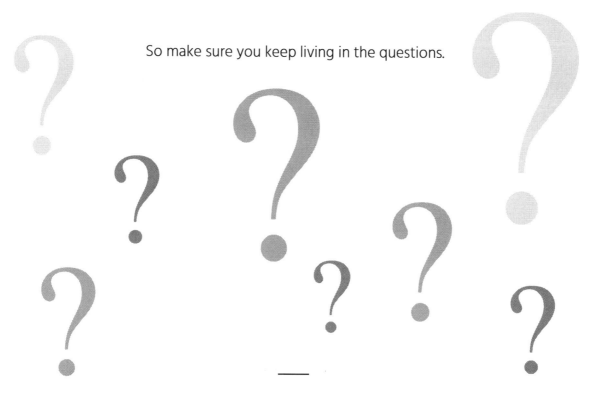

# Morning Practice

What is one thing that you are grateful for right now, something that brings you great joy?

_____

_____

_____

_____

_____

Write out the question you drew from the deck.

_____

_____

_____

Is there one action you are willing to take today that moves you toward your question's answer?

_____

_____

_____

Do a short meditation of 1-2 minutes, just focusing on what's possible, focusing on your question.

Try not to over think it. Throughout your day let the universe do its job.

# Evening Practice

What is one thing you did that brought you joy today?

_____

_____

_____

_____

What one thing did you do today that you would like to do better.

_____

_____

_____

_____

One thing you will commit to do tomorrow that brings joy.

_____

_____

_____

_____

If any answers were discovered you can write them here and/or in the journal page that follows.
Include any coincidences or powerful experiences.

_____

_____

_____

_____

# Journal

# Morning Practice

What is one thing that you are grateful for right now, something that brings you great joy?

Write out the question you drew from the deck.

Is there one action you are willing to take today that moves you toward your question's answer?

Do a short meditation of 1-2 minutes, just focusing on what's possible, focusing on your question.

Try not to over think it. Throughout your day let the universe do its job.

# Evening Practice

What is one thing you did that brought you joy today?

_____

_____

_____

What one thing did you do today that you would like to do better.

_____

_____

_____

One thing you will commit to do tomorrow that brings joy.

_____

_____

_____

If any answers were discovered you can write them here and/or in the journal page that follows.
Include any coincidences or powerful experiences.

_____

_____

_____

# Journal

# Morning Practice

What is one thing that you are grateful for right now, something that brings you great joy?

_____

_____

_____

_____

_____

Write out the question you drew from the deck.

_____

_____

_____

_____

Is there one action you are willing to take today that moves you toward your question's answer?

_____

_____

_____

_____

Do a short meditation of 1-2 minutes, just focusing on what's possible, focusing on your question.

Try not to over think it. Throughout your day let the universe do its job.

---

20

# Evening Practice

What is one thing you did that brought you joy today?

_____

_____

_____

_____

What one thing did you do today that you would like to do better.

_____

_____

_____

_____

One thing you will commit to do tomorrow that brings joy.

_____

_____

_____

_____

If any answers were discovered you can write them here and/or in the journal page that follows.

Include any coincidences or powerful experiences.

_____

_____

_____

_____

# Journal

# Morning Practice

What is one thing that you are grateful for right now, something that brings you great joy?

_____

_____

_____

_____

_____

Write out the question you drew from the deck.

_____

_____

_____

_____

Is there one action you are willing to take today that moves you toward your question's answer?

_____

_____

_____

_____

Do a short meditation of 1-2 minutes, just focusing on what's possible, focusing on your question.

Try not to over think it. Throughout your day let the universe do its job.

# Evening Practice

What is one thing you did that brought you joy today?

_____

_____

_____

What one thing did you do today that you would like to do better.

_____

_____

_____

One thing you will commit to do tomorrow that brings joy.

_____

_____

_____

If any answers were discovered you can write them here and/or in the journal page that follows.

Include any coincidences or powerful experiences.

_____

_____

_____

# Journal

# Morning Practice

What is one thing that you are grateful for right now, something that brings you great joy?

_____

_____

_____

_____

_____

Write out the question you drew from the deck.

_____

_____

_____

_____

Is there one action you are willing to take today that moves you toward your question's answer?

_____

_____

_____

_____

Do a short meditation of 1-2 minutes, just focusing on what's possible, focusing on your question.

Try not to over think it. Throughout your day let the universe do its job.

—

# Evening Practice

What is one thing you did that brought you joy today?

_____

_____

_____

_____

What one thing did you do today that you would like to do better.

_____

_____

_____

_____

One thing you will commit to do tomorrow that brings joy.

_____

_____

_____

_____

If any answers were discovered you can write them here and/or in the journal page that follows.
Include any coincidences or powerful experiences.

_____

_____

_____

_____

# Journal

# Morning Practice

What is one thing that you are grateful for right now, something that brings you great joy?

_____

_____

_____

_____

_____

Write out the question you drew from the deck.

_____

_____

_____

_____

Is there one action you are willing to take today that moves you toward your question's answer?

_____

_____

_____

_____

Do a short meditation of 1-2 minutes, just focusing on what's possible, focusing on your question.

Try not to over think it. Throughout your day let the universe do its job.

# Evening Practice

What is one thing you did that brought you joy today?

_____

_____

_____

_____

What one thing did you do today that you would like to do better.

_____

_____

_____

_____

One thing you will commit to do tomorrow that brings joy.

_____

_____

_____

_____

If any answers were discovered you can write them here and/or in the journal page that follows.
Include any coincidences or powerful experiences.

_____

_____

_____

_____

# Journal

# Morning Practice

What is one thing that you are grateful for right now, something that brings you great joy?

_____

_____

_____

_____

_____

Write out the question you drew from the deck.

_____

_____

_____

_____

Is there one action you are willing to take today that moves you toward your question's answer?

_____

_____

_____

Do a short meditation of 1-2 minutes, just focusing on what's possible, focusing on your question.

Try not to over think it. Throughout your day let the universe do its job.

# Evening Practice

What is one thing you did that brought you joy today?

_____

_____

_____

_____

What one thing did you do today that you would like to do better.

_____

_____

_____

_____

One thing you will commit to do tomorrow that brings joy.

_____

_____

_____

_____

If any answers were discovered you can write them here and/or in the journal page that follows.
Include any coincidences or powerful experiences.

_____

_____

_____

_____

# Journal

# Morning Practice

What is one thing that you are grateful for right now, something that brings you great joy?

_____

_____

_____

_____

Write out the question you drew from the deck.

_____

_____

_____

Is there one action you are willing to take today that moves you toward your question's answer?

_____

_____

_____

Do a short meditation of 1-2 minutes, just focusing on what's possible, focusing on your question.

Try not to over think it. Throughout your day let the universe do its job.

# Evening Practice

What is one thing you did that brought you joy today?

_____

_____

_____

_____

What one thing did you do today that you would like to do better.

_____

_____

_____

_____

One thing you will commit to do tomorrow that brings joy.

_____

_____

_____

_____

If any answers were discovered you can write them here and/or in the journal page that follows.
Include any coincidences or powerful experiences.

_____

_____

_____

_____

# Journal

# Morning Practice

What is one thing that you are grateful for right now, something that brings you great joy?

_____

_____

_____

_____

_____

Write out the question you drew from the deck.

_____

_____

_____

_____

Is there one action you are willing to take today that moves you toward your question's answer?

_____

_____

_____

_____

Do a short meditation of 1-2 minutes, just focusing on what's possible, focusing on your question.

Try not to over think it. Throughout your day let the universe do its job.

# Evening Practice

What is one thing you did that brought you joy today?

_____

_____

_____

What one thing did you do today that you would like to do better.

_____

_____

_____

One thing you will commit to do tomorrow that brings joy.

_____

_____

_____

If any answers were discovered you can write them here and/or in the journal page that follows.

Include any coincidences or powerful experiences.

_____

_____

_____

———

# Journal

# Morning Practice

What is one thing that you are grateful for right now, something that brings you great joy?

_____

_____

_____

_____

_____

Write out the question you drew from the deck.

_____

_____

_____

_____

Is there one action you are willing to take today that moves you toward your question's answer?

_____

_____

_____

Do a short meditation of 1-2 minutes, just focusing on what's possible, focusing on your question.

Try not to over think it. Throughout your day let the universe do its job.

---

# Evening Practice

What is one thing you did that brought you joy today?

_____

_____

_____

_____

What one thing did you do today that you would like to do better.

_____

_____

_____

_____

One thing you will commit to do tomorrow that brings joy.

_____

_____

_____

_____

If any answers were discovered you can write them here and/or in the journal page that follows.
Include any coincidences or powerful experiences.

_____

_____

_____

_____

# Journal

# Morning Practice

What is one thing that you are grateful for right now, something that brings you great joy?

_____

_____

_____

_____

_____

Write out the question you drew from the deck.

_____

_____

_____

Is there one action you are willing to take today that moves you toward your question's answer?

_____

_____

_____

Do a short meditation of 1-2 minutes, just focusing on what's possible, focusing on your question.

Try not to over think it. Throughout your day let the universe do its job.

# Evening Practice

What is one thing you did that brought you joy today?

_____

_____

_____

What one thing did you do today that you would like to do better.

_____

_____

_____

One thing you will commit to do tomorrow that brings joy.

_____

_____

_____

If any answers were discovered you can write them here and/or in the journal page that follows.

Include any coincidences or powerful experiences.

_____

_____

_____

# Journal

# Morning Practice

What is one thing that you are grateful for right now, something that brings you great joy?

Write out the question you drew from the deck.

Is there one action you are willing to take today that moves you toward your question's answer?

Do a short meditation of 1-2 minutes, just focusing on what's possible, focusing on your question.

Try not to over think it. Throughout your day let the universe do its job.

# Evening Practice

What is one thing you did that brought you joy today?

_____

_____

_____

_____

What one thing did you do today that you would like to do better.

_____

_____

_____

_____

One thing you will commit to do tomorrow that brings joy.

_____

_____

_____

_____

If any answers were discovered you can write them here and/or in the journal page that follows.
Include any coincidences or powerful experiences.

_____

_____

_____

_____

# Journal

# Morning Practice

What is one thing that you are grateful for right now, something that brings you great joy?

_____

_____

_____

_____

_____

Write out the question you drew from the deck.

_____

_____

_____

Is there one action you are willing to take today that moves you toward your question's answer?

_____

_____

_____

Do a short meditation of 1-2 minutes, just focusing on what's possible, focusing on your question.

Try not to over think it. Throughout your day let the universe do its job.

# Evening Practice

What is one thing you did that brought you joy today?

_____

_____

_____

What one thing did you do today that you would like to do better.

_____

_____

_____

One thing you will commit to do tomorrow that brings joy.

_____

_____

_____

If any answers were discovered you can write them here and/or in the journal page that follows.
Include any coincidences or powerful experiences.

_____

_____

_____

# Journal

# Morning Practice

What is one thing that you are grateful for right now, something that brings you great joy?

_____

_____

_____

_____

_____

Write out the question you drew from the deck.

_____

_____

_____

Is there one action you are willing to take today that moves you toward your question's answer?

_____

_____

_____

Do a short meditation of 1-2 minutes, just focusing on what's possible, focusing on your question.

Try not to over think it. Throughout your day let the universe do its job.

# Evening Practice

What is one thing you did that brought you joy today?

_____

_____

_____

What one thing did you do today that you would like to do better.

_____

_____

_____

One thing you will commit to do tomorrow that brings joy.

_____

_____

_____

If any answers were discovered you can write them here and/or in the journal page that follows.

Include any coincidences or powerful experiences.

_____

_____

_____

# Journal

# Morning Practice

What is one thing that you are grateful for right now, something that brings you great joy?

_____

_____

_____

_____

_____

Write out the question you drew from the deck.

_____

_____

_____

_____

Is there one action you are willing to take today that moves you toward your question's answer?

_____

_____

_____

_____

Do a short meditation of 1-2 minutes, just focusing on what's possible, focusing on your question.

Try not to over think it. Throughout your day let the universe do its job.

---

# Evening Practice

What is one thing you did that brought you joy today?

_____

_____

_____

_____

What one thing did you do today that you would like to do better.

_____

_____

_____

_____

One thing you will commit to do tomorrow that brings joy.

_____

_____

_____

_____

If any answers were discovered you can write them here and/or in the journal page that follows.

Include any coincidences or powerful experiences.

_____

_____

_____

_____

# Journal

# Morning Practice

What is one thing that you are grateful for right now, something that brings you great joy?

_____

_____

_____

_____

Write out the question you drew from the deck.

_____

_____

_____

Is there one action you are willing to take today that moves you toward your question's answer?

_____

_____

_____

Do a short meditation of 1-2 minutes, just focusing on what's possible, focusing on your question.

Try not to over think it. Throughout your day let the universe do its job.

# Evening Practice

What is one thing you did that brought you joy today?

_____

_____

_____

_____

What one thing did you do today that you would like to do better.

_____

_____

_____

_____

One thing you will commit to do tomorrow that brings joy.

_____

_____

_____

_____

If any answers were discovered you can write them here and/or in the journal page that follows.
Include any coincidences or powerful experiences.

_____

_____

_____

_____

# Journal

# Morning Practice

What is one thing that you are grateful for right now, something that brings you great joy?

_____

_____

_____

_____

_____

Write out the question you drew from the deck.

_____

_____

_____

_____

Is there one action you are willing to take today that moves you toward your question's answer?

_____

_____

_____

_____

Do a short meditation of 1-2 minutes, just focusing on what's possible, focusing on your question.
Try not to over think it. Throughout your day let the universe do its job.

———

# Evening Practice

What is one thing you did that brought you joy today?

_____

_____

_____

_____

What one thing did you do today that you would like to do better.

_____

_____

_____

_____

One thing you will commit to do tomorrow that brings joy.

_____

_____

_____

_____

If any answers were discovered you can write them here and/or in the journal page that follows.
Include any coincidences or powerful experiences.

_____

_____

_____

_____

# Journal

# Morning Practice

What is one thing that you are grateful for right now, something that brings you great joy?

_____

_____

_____

_____

_____

Write out the question you drew from the deck.

_____

_____

_____

_____

Is there one action you are willing to take today that moves you toward your question's answer?

_____

_____

_____

_____

Do a short meditation of 1-2 minutes, just focusing on what's possible, focusing on your question.
Try not to over think it. Throughout your day let the universe do its job.

# Evening Practice

What is one thing you did that brought you joy today?

_____

_____

_____

What one thing did you do today that you would like to do better.

_____

_____

_____

One thing you will commit to do tomorrow that brings joy.

_____

_____

_____

If any answers were discovered you can write them here and/or in the journal page that follows.

Include any coincidences or powerful experiences.

_____

_____

_____

# Journal

# Morning Practice

What is one thing that you are grateful for right now, something that brings you great joy?

_____

_____

_____

_____

_____

Write out the question you drew from the deck.

_____

_____

_____

Is there one action you are willing to take today that moves you toward your question's answer?

_____

_____

_____

Do a short meditation of 1-2 minutes, just focusing on what's possible, focusing on your question.

Try not to over think it. Throughout your day let the universe do its job.

# Evening Practice

What is one thing you did that brought you joy today?

_____

_____

_____

What one thing did you do today that you would like to do better.

_____

_____

_____

One thing you will commit to do tomorrow that brings joy.

_____

_____

_____

If any answers were discovered you can write them here and/or in the journal page that follows.
Include any coincidences or powerful experiences.

_____

_____

_____

# Journal

# Morning Practice

What is one thing that you are grateful for right now, something that brings you great joy?

_____

_____

_____

_____

_____

Write out the question you drew from the deck.

_____

_____

_____

_____

Is there one action you are willing to take today that moves you toward your question's answer?

_____

_____

_____

_____

Do a short meditation of 1-2 minutes, just focusing on what's possible, focusing on your question.

Try not to over think it. Throughout your day let the universe do its job.

—

# Evening Practice

What is one thing you did that brought you joy today?

_____

_____

_____

What one thing did you do today that you would like to do better.

_____

_____

_____

One thing you will commit to do tomorrow that brings joy.

_____

_____

_____

If any answers were discovered you can write them here and/or in the journal page that follows.
Include any coincidences or powerful experiences.

_____

_____

_____

# Journal

# Morning Practice

What is one thing that you are grateful for right now, something that brings you great joy?

Write out the question you drew from the deck.

Is there one action you are willing to take today that moves you toward your question's answer?

Do a short meditation of 1-2 minutes, just focusing on what's possible, focusing on your question.

Try not to over think it. Throughout your day let the universe do its job.

# Evening Practice

What is one thing you did that brought you joy today?

_____

_____

_____

What one thing did you do today that you would like to do better.

_____

_____

_____

One thing you will commit to do tomorrow that brings joy.

_____

_____

_____

If any answers were discovered you can write them here and/or in the journal page that follows.

Include any coincidences or powerful experiences.

_____

_____

_____

# Journal

# Morning Practice

What is one thing that you are grateful for right now, something that brings you great joy?

_____

_____

_____

_____

_____

Write out the question you drew from the deck.

_____

_____

_____

_____

Is there one action you are willing to take today that moves you toward your question's answer?

_____

_____

_____

Do a short meditation of 1-2 minutes, just focusing on what's possible, focusing on your question.

Try not to over think it. Throughout your day let the universe do its job.

# Evening Practice

What is one thing you did that brought you joy today?

_____

_____

_____

What one thing did you do today that you would like to do better.

_____

_____

_____

One thing you will commit to do tomorrow that brings joy.

_____

_____

_____

If any answers were discovered you can write them here and/or in the journal page that follows.

Include any coincidences or powerful experiences.

_____

_____

_____

# Journal

# Morning Practice

What is one thing that you are grateful for right now, something that brings you great joy?

---

Write out the question you drew from the deck.

---

Is there one action you are willing to take today that moves you toward your question's answer?

---

Do a short meditation of 1-2 minutes, just focusing on what's possible, focusing on your question.

Try not to over think it. Throughout your day let the universe do its job.

# Evening Practice

What is one thing you did that brought you joy today?

_____

_____

_____

What one thing did you do today that you would like to do better.

_____

_____

_____

One thing you will commit to do tomorrow that brings joy.

_____

_____

_____

If any answers were discovered you can write them here and/or in the journal page that follows.

Include any coincidences or powerful experiences.

_____

_____

_____

# Journal

# Morning Practice

What is one thing that you are grateful for right now, something that brings you great joy?

_____

_____

_____

_____

_____

Write out the question you drew from the deck.

_____

_____

_____

Is there one action you are willing to take today that moves you toward your question's answer?

_____

_____

_____

Do a short meditation of 1-2 minutes, just focusing on what's possible, focusing on your question.
Try not to over think it. Throughout your day let the universe do its job.

# Evening Practice

What is one thing you did that brought you joy today?

_____

_____

_____

_____

What one thing did you do today that you would like to do better.

_____

_____

_____

_____

One thing you will commit to do tomorrow that brings joy.

_____

_____

_____

_____

If any answers were discovered you can write them here and/or in the journal page that follows.
Include any coincidences or powerful experiences.

_____

_____

_____

_____

# Journal

# Morning Practice

What is one thing that you are grateful for right now, something that brings you great joy?

_____

_____

_____

_____

_____

Write out the question you drew from the deck.

_____

_____

_____

Is there one action you are willing to take today that moves you toward your question's answer?

_____

_____

_____

Do a short meditation of 1-2 minutes, just focusing on what's possible, focusing on your question.

Try not to over think it. Throughout your day let the universe do its job.

# Evening Practice

What is one thing you did that brought you joy today?

_____

_____

_____

What one thing did you do today that you would like to do better.

_____

_____

_____

One thing you will commit to do tomorrow that brings joy.

_____

_____

_____

If any answers were discovered you can write them here and/or in the journal page that follows.
Include any coincidences or powerful experiences.

_____

_____

_____

# Journal

# Morning Practice

What is one thing that you are grateful for right now, something that brings you great joy?

_____

_____

_____

_____

_____

Write out the question you drew from the deck.

_____

_____

_____

Is there one action you are willing to take today that moves you toward your question's answer?

_____

_____

_____

Do a short meditation of 1-2 minutes, just focusing on what's possible, focusing on your question.

Try not to over think it. Throughout your day let the universe do its job.

# Evening Practice

What is one thing you did that brought you joy today?

_____

_____

_____

What one thing did you do today that you would like to do better.

_____

_____

_____

One thing you will commit to do tomorrow that brings joy.

_____

_____

_____

If any answers were discovered you can write them here and/or in the journal page that follows.
Include any coincidences or powerful experiences.

_____

_____

_____

# Journal

# Morning Practice

What is one thing that you are grateful for right now, something that brings you great joy?

_____

_____

_____

_____

_____

Write out the question you drew from the deck.

_____

_____

_____

Is there one action you are willing to take today that moves you toward your question's answer?

_____

_____

_____

Do a short meditation of 1-2 minutes, just focusing on what's possible, focusing on your question.

Try not to over think it. Throughout your day let the universe do its job.

# Evening Practice

What is one thing you did that brought you joy today?

_____

_____

_____

What one thing did you do today that you would like to do better.

_____

_____

_____

One thing you will commit to do tomorrow that brings joy.

_____

_____

_____

If any answers were discovered you can write them here and/or in the journal page that follows.
Include any coincidences or powerful experiences.

_____

_____

_____

# Journal

# Morning Practice

What is one thing that you are grateful for right now, something that brings you great joy?

Write out the question you drew from the deck.

Is there one action you are willing to take today that moves you toward your question's answer?

Do a short meditation of 1-2 minutes, just focusing on what's possible, focusing on your question.

Try not to over think it. Throughout your day let the universe do its job.

# Evening Practice

What is one thing you did that brought you joy today?

_____

_____

_____

What one thing did you do today that you would like to do better.

_____

_____

_____

One thing you will commit to do tomorrow that brings joy.

_____

_____

_____

If any answers were discovered you can write them here and/or in the journal page that follows.
Include any coincidences or powerful experiences.

_____

_____

_____

# Journal

# Morning Practice

What is one thing that you are grateful for right now, something that brings you great joy?

Write out the question you drew from the deck.

Is there one action you are willing to take today that moves you toward your question's answer?

Do a short meditation of 1-2 minutes, just focusing on what's possible, focusing on your question.

Try not to over think it. Throughout your day let the universe do its job.

# Evening Practice

What is one thing you did that brought you joy today?

_____

_____

_____

What one thing did you do today that you would like to do better.

_____

_____

_____

One thing you will commit to do tomorrow that brings joy.

_____

_____

_____

If any answers were discovered you can write them here and/or in the journal page that follows.
Include any coincidences or powerful experiences.

_____

_____

_____

# Journal

# Morning Practice

What is one thing that you are grateful for right now, something that brings you great joy?

_____

_____

_____

_____

_____

Write out the question you drew from the deck.

_____

_____

_____

_____

Is there one action you are willing to take today that moves you toward your question's answer?

_____

_____

_____

_____

Do a short meditation of 1-2 minutes, just focusing on what's possible, focusing on your question.

Try not to over think it. Throughout your day let the universe do its job.

—

# Evening Practice

What is one thing you did that brought you joy today?

_____

_____

_____

What one thing did you do today that you would like to do better.

_____

_____

_____

One thing you will commit to do tomorrow that brings joy.

_____

_____

_____

If any answers were discovered you can write them here and/or in the journal page that follows.
Include any coincidences or powerful experiences.

_____

_____

_____

# Journal

# Morning Practice

What is one thing that you are grateful for right now, something that brings you great joy?

Write out the question you drew from the deck.

Is there one action you are willing to take today that moves you toward your question's answer?

Do a short meditation of 1-2 minutes, just focusing on what's possible, focusing on your question.

Try not to over think it. Throughout your day let the universe do its job.

# Evening Practice

What is one thing you did that brought you joy today?

_____

_____

_____

_____

What one thing did you do today that you would like to do better.

_____

_____

_____

_____

One thing you will commit to do tomorrow that brings joy.

_____

_____

_____

_____

If any answers were discovered you can write them here and/or in the journal page that follows.

Include any coincidences or powerful experiences.

_____

_____

_____

_____

# Journal

# Morning Practice

What is one thing that you are grateful for right now, something that brings you great joy?

_____

_____

_____

_____

_____

Write out the question you drew from the deck.

_____

_____

_____

_____

Is there one action you are willing to take today that moves you toward your question's answer?

_____

_____

_____

_____

Do a short meditation of 1-2 minutes, just focusing on what's possible, focusing on your question.

Try not to over think it. Throughout your day let the universe do its job.

# Evening Practice

What is one thing you did that brought you joy today?

_____

_____

_____

What one thing did you do today that you would like to do better.

_____

_____

_____

One thing you will commit to do tomorrow that brings joy.

_____

_____

_____

If any answers were discovered you can write them here and/or in the journal page that follows.
Include any coincidences or powerful experiences.

_____

_____

_____

# Journal

# Morning Practice

What is one thing that you are grateful for right now, something that brings you great joy?

_____

_____

_____

_____

_____

Write out the question you drew from the deck.

_____

_____

_____

Is there one action you are willing to take today that moves you toward your question's answer?

_____

_____

_____

Do a short meditation of 1-2 minutes, just focusing on what's possible, focusing on your question.

Try not to over think it. Throughout your day let the universe do its job.

# Evening Practice

What is one thing you did that brought you joy today?

_____

_____

_____

What one thing did you do today that you would like to do better.

_____

_____

_____

One thing you will commit to do tomorrow that brings joy.

_____

_____

_____

If any answers were discovered you can write them here and/or in the journal page that follows.
Include any coincidences or powerful experiences.

_____

_____

_____

# Journal

# Morning Practice

What is one thing that you are grateful for right now, something that brings you great joy?

_____

_____

_____

_____

Write out the question you drew from the deck.

_____

_____

_____

Is there one action you are willing to take today that moves you toward your question's answer?

_____

_____

_____

Do a short meditation of 1-2 minutes, just focusing on what's possible, focusing on your question.

Try not to over think it. Throughout your day let the universe do its job.

# Evening Practice

What is one thing you did that brought you joy today?

_____

_____

_____

What one thing did you do today that you would like to do better.

_____

_____

_____

One thing you will commit to do tomorrow that brings joy.

_____

_____

_____

If any answers were discovered you can write them here and/or in the journal page that follows.
Include any coincidences or powerful experiences.

_____

_____

_____

# Journal

# Morning Practice

What is one thing that you are grateful for right now, something that brings you great joy?

---

---

---

---

---

Write out the question you drew from the deck.

---

---

---

---

Is there one action you are willing to take today that moves you toward your question's answer?

---

---

---

---

Do a short meditation of 1-2 minutes, just focusing on what's possible, focusing on your question.

Try not to over think it. Throughout your day let the universe do its job.

# Evening Practice

What is one thing you did that brought you joy today?

_____

_____

_____

_____

What one thing did you do today that you would like to do better.

_____

_____

_____

_____

One thing you will commit to do tomorrow that brings joy.

_____

_____

_____

_____

If any answers were discovered you can write them here and/or in the journal page that follows.

Include any coincidences or powerful experiences.

_____

_____

_____

_____

# Journal

# Morning Practice

What is one thing that you are grateful for right now, something that brings you great joy?

Write out the question you drew from the deck.

Is there one action you are willing to take today that moves you toward your question's answer?

Do a short meditation of 1-2 minutes, just focusing on what's possible, focusing on your question.

Try not to over think it. Throughout your day let the universe do its job.

# Evening Practice

What is one thing you did that brought you joy today?

_____

_____

_____

What one thing did you do today that you would like to do better.

_____

_____

_____

One thing you will commit to do tomorrow that brings joy.

_____

_____

If any answers were discovered you can write them here and/or in the journal page that follows.
Include any coincidences or powerful experiences.

_____

_____

_____

# Journal

# Morning Practice

What is one thing that you are grateful for right now, something that brings you great joy?

Write out the question you drew from the deck.

Is there one action you are willing to take today that moves you toward your question's answer?

Do a short meditation of 1-2 minutes, just focusing on what's possible, focusing on your question.

Try not to over think it. Throughout your day let the universe do its job.

# Evening Practice

What is one thing you did that brought you joy today?

_____

_____

_____

What one thing did you do today that you would like to do better.

_____

_____

_____

One thing you will commit to do tomorrow that brings joy.

_____

_____

_____

If any answers were discovered you can write them here and/or in the journal page that follows.
Include any coincidences or powerful experiences.

_____

_____

_____

_____

# Journal

# Morning Practice

What is one thing that you are grateful for right now, something that brings you great joy?

_____

_____

_____

_____

_____

Write out the question you drew from the deck.

_____

_____

_____

_____

Is there one action you are willing to take today that moves you toward your question's answer?

_____

_____

_____

_____

Do a short meditation of 1-2 minutes, just focusing on what's possible, focusing on your question.

Try not to over think it. Throughout your day let the universe do its job.

# Evening Practice

What is one thing you did that brought you joy today?

_____

_____

_____

What one thing did you do today that you would like to do better.

_____

_____

_____

One thing you will commit to do tomorrow that brings joy.

_____

_____

_____

If any answers were discovered you can write them here and/or in the journal page that follows.
Include any coincidences or powerful experiences.

_____

_____

_____

# Journal

# Morning Practice

What is one thing that you are grateful for right now, something that brings you great joy?

_____

_____

_____

_____

_____

Write out the question you drew from the deck.

_____

_____

_____

Is there one action you are willing to take today that moves you toward your question's answer?

_____

_____

_____

Do a short meditation of 1-2 minutes, just focusing on what's possible, focusing on your question.

Try not to over think it. Throughout your day let the universe do its job.

---

# Evening Practice

What is one thing you did that brought you joy today?

_____

_____

_____

What one thing did you do today that you would like to do better.

_____

_____

_____

One thing you will commit to do tomorrow that brings joy.

_____

_____

_____

If any answers were discovered you can write them here and/or in the journal page that follows.
Include any coincidences or powerful experiences.

_____

_____

_____

# Morning Practice

What is one thing that you are grateful for right now, something that brings you great joy?

_____

_____

_____

_____

_____

Write out the question you drew from the deck.

_____

_____

_____

_____

Is there one action you are willing to take today that moves you toward your question's answer?

_____

_____

_____

Do a short meditation of 1-2 minutes, just focusing on what's possible, focusing on your question.

Try not to over think it. Throughout your day let the universe do its job.

# Evening Practice

What is one thing you did that brought you joy today?

_____

_____

_____

What one thing did you do today that you would like to do better.

_____

_____

_____

One thing you will commit to do tomorrow that brings joy.

_____

_____

_____

If any answers were discovered you can write them here and/or in the journal page that follows.
Include any coincidences or powerful experiences.

_____

_____

_____

# Journal

# Morning Practice

What is one thing that you are grateful for right now, something that brings you great joy?

_____

_____

_____

_____

_____

Write out the question you drew from the deck.

_____

_____

_____

Is there one action you are willing to take today that moves you toward your question's answer?

_____

_____

_____

Do a short meditation of 1-2 minutes, just focusing on what's possible, focusing on your question.

Try not to over think it. Throughout your day let the universe do its job.

# Evening Practice

What is one thing you did that brought you joy today?

_____

_____

_____

_____

What one thing did you do today that you would like to do better.

_____

_____

_____

_____

One thing you will commit to do tomorrow that brings joy.

_____

_____

_____

_____

If any answers were discovered you can write them here and/or in the journal page that follows.
Include any coincidences or powerful experiences.

_____

_____

_____

_____

# Journal

# Morning Practice

What is one thing that you are grateful for right now, something that brings you great joy?

_____

_____

_____

_____

_____

Write out the question you drew from the deck.

_____

_____

_____

_____

Is there one action you are willing to take today that moves you toward your question's answer?

_____

_____

_____

_____

Do a short meditation of 1-2 minutes, just focusing on what's possible, focusing on your question.

Try not to over think it. Throughout your day let the universe do its job.

# Evening Practice

What is one thing you did that brought you joy today?

_____

_____

_____

_____

What one thing did you do today that you would like to do better.

_____

_____

_____

_____

One thing you will commit to do tomorrow that brings joy.

_____

_____

_____

_____

If any answers were discovered you can write them here and/or in the journal page that follows.
Include any coincidences or powerful experiences.

_____

_____

_____

_____

# Journal

# Morning Practice

What is one thing that you are grateful for right now, something that brings you great joy?

_____

_____

_____

_____

_____

Write out the question you drew from the deck.

_____

_____

_____

Is there one action you are willing to take today that moves you toward your question's answer?

_____

_____

_____

Do a short meditation of 1-2 minutes, just focusing on what's possible, focusing on your question.

Try not to over think it. Throughout your day let the universe do its job.

# Evening Practice

What is one thing you did that brought you joy today?

_____

_____

_____

What one thing did you do today that you would like to do better.

_____

_____

_____

One thing you will commit to do tomorrow that brings joy.

_____

_____

_____

If any answers were discovered you can write them here and/or in the journal page that follows.

Include any coincidences or powerful experiences.

_____

_____

_____

# Journal

# Morning Practice

What is one thing that you are grateful for right now, something that brings you great joy?

_____

_____

_____

_____

_____

Write out the question you drew from the deck.

_____

_____

_____

_____

Is there one action you are willing to take today that moves you toward your question's answer?

_____

_____

_____

_____

Do a short meditation of 1-2 minutes, just focusing on what's possible, focusing on your question.

Try not to over think it. Throughout your day let the universe do its job.

# Evening Practice

What is one thing you did that brought you joy today?

_____

_____

_____

_____

What one thing did you do today that you would like to do better.

_____

_____

_____

_____

One thing you will commit to do tomorrow that brings joy.

_____

_____

_____

_____

If any answers were discovered you can write them here and/or in the journal page that follows.
Include any coincidences or powerful experiences.

_____

_____

_____

_____

# Journal

# Morning Practice

What is one thing that you are grateful for right now, something that brings you great joy?

_____

_____

_____

_____

_____

Write out the question you drew from the deck.

_____

_____

_____

Is there one action you are willing to take today that moves you toward your question's answer?

_____

_____

_____

Do a short meditation of 1-2 minutes, just focusing on what's possible, focusing on your question.

Try not to over think it. Throughout your day let the universe do its job.

# Evening Practice

What is one thing you did that brought you joy today?

_____

_____

_____

What one thing did you do today that you would like to do better.

_____

_____

_____

One thing you will commit to do tomorrow that brings joy.

_____

_____

_____

If any answers were discovered you can write them here and/or in the journal page that follows.
Include any coincidences or powerful experiences.

_____

_____

_____

# Journal

# Morning Practice

What is one thing that you are grateful for right now, something that brings you great joy?

_____

_____

_____

_____

_____

Write out the question you drew from the deck.

_____

_____

_____

Is there one action you are willing to take today that moves you toward your question's answer?

_____

_____

_____

Do a short meditation of 1-2 minutes, just focusing on what's possible, focusing on your question.

Try not to over think it. Throughout your day let the universe do its job.

# Evening Practice

What is one thing you did that brought you joy today?

What one thing did you do today that you would like to do better.

One thing you will commit to do tomorrow that brings joy.

If any answers were discovered you can write them here and/or in the journal page that follows.

Include any coincidences or powerful experiences.

# Journal

# Morning Practice

What is one thing that you are grateful for right now, something that brings you great joy?

_____

_____

_____

_____

Write out the question you drew from the deck.

_____

_____

_____

Is there one action you are willing to take today that moves you toward your question's answer?

_____

_____

_____

Do a short meditation of 1-2 minutes, just focusing on what's possible, focusing on your question.

Try not to over think it. Throughout your day let the universe do its job.

# Evening Practice

What is one thing you did that brought you joy today?

_____

_____

_____

What one thing did you do today that you would like to do better.

_____

_____

_____

One thing you will commit to do tomorrow that brings joy.

_____

_____

_____

If any answers were discovered you can write them here and/or in the journal page that follows.
Include any coincidences or powerful experiences.

_____

_____

_____

# Journal

# Morning Practice

What is one thing that you are grateful for right now, something that brings you great joy?

Write out the question you drew from the deck.

Is there one action you are willing to take today that moves you toward your question's answer?

Do a short meditation of 1-2 minutes, just focusing on what's possible, focusing on your question.

Try not to over think it. Throughout your day let the universe do its job.

# Evening Practice

What is one thing you did that brought you joy today?

_____

_____

_____

What one thing did you do today that you would like to do better.

_____

_____

_____

One thing you will commit to do tomorrow that brings joy.

_____

_____

_____

If any answers were discovered you can write them here and/or in the journal page that follows.
Include any coincidences or powerful experiences.

_____

_____

_____

# Journal

# Morning Practice

What is one thing that you are grateful for right now, something that brings you great joy?

Write out the question you drew from the deck.

Is there one action you are willing to take today that moves you toward your question's answer?

Do a short meditation of 1-2 minutes, just focusing on what's possible, focusing on your question.

Try not to over think it. Throughout your day let the universe do its job.

# Evening Practice

What is one thing you did that brought you joy today?

_____

_____

_____

What one thing did you do today that you would like to do better.

_____

_____

_____

One thing you will commit to do tomorrow that brings joy.

_____

_____

_____

If any answers were discovered you can write them here and/or in the journal page that follows. Include any coincidences or powerful experiences.

_____

_____

_____

# Journal

# Morning Practice

What is one thing that you are grateful for right now, something that brings you great joy?

_____

_____

_____

_____

_____

Write out the question you drew from the deck.

_____

_____

_____

Is there one action you are willing to take today that moves you toward your question's answer?

_____

_____

_____

Do a short meditation of 1-2 minutes, just focusing on what's possible, focusing on your question.

Try not to over think it. Throughout your day let the universe do its job.

# Evening Practice

What is one thing you did that brought you joy today?

_____

_____

_____

_____

What one thing did you do today that you would like to do better.

_____

_____

_____

_____

One thing you will commit to do tomorrow that brings joy.

_____

_____

_____

_____

If any answers were discovered you can write them here and/or in the journal page that follows.
Include any coincidences or powerful experiences.

_____

_____

_____

_____

# Journal

# Morning Practice

What is one thing that you are grateful for right now, something that brings you great joy?

_____

_____

_____

_____

_____

Write out the question you drew from the deck.

_____

_____

_____

Is there one action you are willing to take today that moves you toward your question's answer?

_____

_____

_____

Do a short meditation of 1-2 minutes, just focusing on what's possible, focusing on your question.

Try not to over think it. Throughout your day let the universe do its job.

---

# Evening Practice

What is one thing you did that brought you joy today?

_____

_____

_____

What one thing did you do today that you would like to do better.

_____

_____

_____

One thing you will commit to do tomorrow that brings joy.

_____

_____

_____

If any answers were discovered you can write them here and/or in the journal page that follows.
Include any coincidences or powerful experiences.

_____

_____

_____

# Journal

# Morning Practice

What is one thing that you are grateful for right now, something that brings you great joy?

_____

_____

_____

_____

_____

Write out the question you drew from the deck.

_____

_____

_____

_____

Is there one action you are willing to take today that moves you toward your question's answer?

_____

_____

_____

_____

Do a short meditation of 1-2 minutes, just focusing on what's possible, focusing on your question.

Try not to over think it. Throughout your day let the universe do its job.

# Evening Practice

What is one thing you did that brought you joy today?

_____

_____

_____

_____

What one thing did you do today that you would like to do better.

_____

_____

_____

_____

One thing you will commit to do tomorrow that brings joy.

_____

_____

_____

_____

If any answers were discovered you can write them here and/or in the journal page that follows.

Include any coincidences or powerful experiences.

_____

_____

_____

_____

# Journal

# Morning Practice

What is one thing that you are grateful for right now, something that brings you great joy?

_____

_____

_____

_____

_____

Write out the question you drew from the deck.

_____

_____

_____

Is there one action you are willing to take today that moves you toward your question's answer?

_____

_____

_____

Do a short meditation of 1-2 minutes, just focusing on what's possible, focusing on your question.
Try not to over think it. Throughout your day let the universe do its job.

# Evening Practice

What is one thing you did that brought you joy today?

_____

_____

_____

What one thing did you do today that you would like to do better.

_____

_____

_____

One thing you will commit to do tomorrow that brings joy.

_____

_____

_____

If any answers were discovered you can write them here and/or in the journal page that follows.

Include any coincidences or powerful experiences.

_____

_____

_____

# Journal

# Morning Practice

What is one thing that you are grateful for right now, something that brings you great joy?

_____

_____

_____

_____

_____

Write out the question you drew from the deck.

_____

_____

_____

Is there one action you are willing to take today that moves you toward your question's answer?

_____

_____

_____

Do a short meditation of 1-2 minutes, just focusing on what's possible, focusing on your question.

Try not to over think it. Throughout your day let the universe do its job.

What is one thing you did that brought you joy today?

_____

_____

_____

What one thing did you do today that you would like to do better.

_____

_____

_____

One thing you will commit to do tomorrow that brings joy.

_____

_____

_____

If any answers were discovered you can write them here and/or in the journal page that follows.
Include any coincidences or powerful experiences.

_____

_____

_____

# Evening Practice

What is one thing you did that brought you joy today?

_____

_____

_____

What one thing did you do today that you would like to do better.

_____

_____

_____

One thing you will commit to do tomorrow that brings joy.

_____

_____

_____

If any answers were discovered you can write them here and/or in the journal page that follows.
Include any coincidences or powerful experiences.

_____

_____

_____

# Journal

# Morning Practice

What is one thing that you are grateful for right now, something that brings you great joy?

_____

_____

_____

_____

_____

Write out the question you drew from the deck.

_____

_____

_____

_____

Is there one action you are willing to take today that moves you toward your question's answer?

_____

_____

_____

Do a short meditation of 1-2 minutes, just focusing on what's possible, focusing on your question.

Try not to over think it. Throughout your day let the universe do its job.

# Evening Practice

What is one thing you did that brought you joy today?

_____

_____

_____

What one thing did you do today that you would like to do better.

_____

_____

_____

One thing you will commit to do tomorrow that brings joy.

_____

_____

_____

If any answers were discovered you can write them here and/or in the journal page that follows.
Include any coincidences or powerful experiences.

_____

_____

_____

# Journal

# Morning Practice

What is one thing that you are grateful for right now, something that brings you great joy?

Write out the question you drew from the deck.

Is there one action you are willing to take today that moves you toward your question's answer?

Do a short meditation of 1-2 minutes, just focusing on what's possible, focusing on your question.

Try not to over think it. Throughout your day let the universe do its job.

# Evening Practice

What is one thing you did that brought you joy today?

_____

_____

_____

_____

What one thing did you do today that you would like to do better.

_____

_____

_____

_____

One thing you will commit to do tomorrow that brings joy.

_____

_____

_____

_____

If any answers were discovered you can write them here and/or in the journal page that follows.
Include any coincidences or powerful experiences.

_____

_____

_____

_____

# Journal

# Morning Practice

What is one thing that you are grateful for right now, something that brings you great joy?

Write out the question you drew from the deck.

Is there one action you are willing to take today that moves you toward your question's answer?

Do a short meditation of 1-2 minutes, just focusing on what's possible, focusing on your question.

Try not to over think it. Throughout your day let the universe do its job.

# Evening Practice

What is one thing you did that brought you joy today?

_____

_____

_____

What one thing did you do today that you would like to do better.

_____

_____

_____

One thing you will commit to do tomorrow that brings joy.

_____

_____

_____

If any answers were discovered you can write them here and/or in the journal page that follows.
Include any coincidences or powerful experiences.

_____

_____

_____

# Journal

# Morning Practice

What is one thing that you are grateful for right now, something that brings you great joy?

_____

_____

_____

_____

_____

Write out the question you drew from the deck.

_____

_____

_____

_____

Is there one action you are willing to take today that moves you toward your question's answer?

_____

_____

_____

Do a short meditation of 1-2 minutes, just focusing on what's possible, focusing on your question.

Try not to over think it. Throughout your day let the universe do its job.

# Evening Practice

What is one thing you did that brought you joy today?

What one thing did you do today that you would like to do better.

One thing you will commit to do tomorrow that brings joy.

If any answers were discovered you can write them here and/or in the journal page that follows.

Include any coincidences or powerful experiences.

# Journal

# Morning Practice

---

What is one thing that you are grateful for right now, something that brings you great joy?

_____

_____

_____

_____

_____

Write out the question you drew from the deck.

_____

_____

_____

Is there one action you are willing to take today that moves you toward your question's answer?

_____

_____

_____

Do a short meditation of 1-2 minutes, just focusing on what's possible, focusing on your question.

Try not to over think it. Throughout your day let the universe do its job.

# Evening Practice

What is one thing you did that brought you joy today?

_____

_____

_____

What one thing did you do today that you would like to do better.

_____

_____

_____

One thing you will commit to do tomorrow that brings joy.

_____

_____

_____

If any answers were discovered you can write them here and/or in the journal page that follows.

Include any coincidences or powerful experiences.

_____

_____

_____

# Journal

# Morning Practice

What is one thing that you are grateful for right now, something that brings you great joy?

_____

_____

_____

_____

_____

Write out the question you drew from the deck.

_____

_____

_____

_____

Is there one action you are willing to take today that moves you toward your question's answer?

_____

_____

_____

Do a short meditation of 1-2 minutes, just focusing on what's possible, focusing on your question.

Try not to over think it. Throughout your day let the universe do its job.

---

# Evening Practice

What is one thing you did that brought you joy today?

_____

_____

_____

_____

What one thing did you do today that you would like to do better.

_____

_____

_____

_____

One thing you will commit to do tomorrow that brings joy.

_____

_____

_____

_____

If any answers were discovered you can write them here and/or in the journal page that follows.
Include any coincidences or powerful experiences.

_____

_____

_____

_____

# Journal

# Morning Practice

What is one thing that you are grateful for right now, something that brings you great joy?

_____

_____

_____

_____

Write out the question you drew from the deck.

_____

_____

_____

Is there one action you are willing to take today that moves you toward your question's answer?

_____

_____

_____

Do a short meditation of 1-2 minutes, just focusing on what's possible, focusing on your question.

Try not to over think it. Throughout your day let the universe do its job.

# Evening Practice

What is one thing you did that brought you joy today?

_____

_____

_____

_____

What one thing did you do today that you would like to do better.

_____

_____

_____

_____

One thing you will commit to do tomorrow that brings joy.

_____

_____

_____

_____

If any answers were discovered you can write them here and/or in the journal page that follows.
Include any coincidences or powerful experiences.

_____

_____

_____

_____

# Journal

# Morning Practice

What is one thing that you are grateful for right now, something that brings you great joy?

_____

_____

_____

_____

_____

Write out the question you drew from the deck.

_____

_____

_____

_____

Is there one action you are willing to take today that moves you toward your question's answer?

_____

_____

_____

Do a short meditation of 1-2 minutes, just focusing on what's possible, focusing on your question.

Try not to over think it. Throughout your day let the universe do its job.

---

# Evening Practice

What is one thing you did that brought you joy today?

_____

_____

_____

What one thing did you do today that you would like to do better.

_____

_____

_____

One thing you will commit to do tomorrow that brings joy.

_____

_____

_____

If any answers were discovered you can write them here and/or in the journal page that follows.

Include any coincidences or powerful experiences.

_____

_____

_____

# Journal

# Morning Practice

What is one thing that you are grateful for right now, something that brings you great joy?

_____

_____

_____

_____

_____

Write out the question you drew from the deck.

_____

_____

_____

Is there one action you are willing to take today that moves you toward your question's answer?

_____

_____

_____

Do a short meditation of 1-2 minutes, just focusing on what's possible, focusing on your question.

Try not to over think it. Throughout your day let the universe do its job.

# Evening Practice

What is one thing you did that brought you joy today?

_____

_____

_____

What one thing did you do today that you would like to do better.

_____

_____

_____

One thing you will commit to do tomorrow that brings joy.

_____

_____

_____

If any answers were discovered you can write them here and/or in the journal page that follows.
Include any coincidences or powerful experiences.

_____

_____

_____

# Journal

# Morning Practice

What is one thing that you are grateful for right now, something that brings you great joy?

_____

_____

_____

_____

_____

Write out the question you drew from the deck.

_____

_____

_____

_____

Is there one action you are willing to take today that moves you toward your question's answer?

_____

_____

_____

_____

Do a short meditation of 1-2 minutes, just focusing on what's possible, focusing on your question.

Try not to over think it. Throughout your day let the universe do its job.

# Evening Practice

What is one thing you did that brought you joy today?

_____

_____

_____

What one thing did you do today that you would like to do better.

_____

_____

_____

One thing you will commit to do tomorrow that brings joy.

_____

_____

_____

If any answers were discovered you can write them here and/or in the journal page that follows.
Include any coincidences or powerful experiences.

_____

_____

_____

# Journal

# Morning Practice

What is one thing that you are grateful for right now, something that brings you great joy?

_____

_____

_____

_____

_____

Write out the question you drew from the deck.

_____

_____

_____

_____

Is there one action you are willing to take today that moves you toward your question's answer?

_____

_____

_____

Do a short meditation of 1-2 minutes, just focusing on what's possible, focusing on your question.

Try not to over think it. Throughout your day let the universe do its job.

# Evening Practice

What is one thing you did that brought you joy today?

_____

_____

_____

What one thing did you do today that you would like to do better.

_____

_____

_____

One thing you will commit to do tomorrow that brings joy.

_____

_____

_____

If any answers were discovered you can write them here and/or in the journal page that follows.
Include any coincidences or powerful experiences.

_____

_____

_____

# Journal

# Morning Practice

What is one thing that you are grateful for right now, something that brings you great joy?

_____

_____

_____

_____

_____

Write out the question you drew from the deck.

_____

_____

_____

Is there one action you are willing to take today that moves you toward your question's answer?

_____

_____

_____

Do a short meditation of 1-2 minutes, just focusing on what's possible, focusing on your question.

Try not to over think it. Throughout your day let the universe do its job.

# Evening Practice

What is one thing you did that brought you joy today?

_____

_____

_____

What one thing did you do today that you would like to do better.

_____

_____

_____

One thing you will commit to do tomorrow that brings joy.

_____

_____

_____

If any answers were discovered you can write them here and/or in the journal page that follows.
Include any coincidences or powerful experiences.

_____

_____

_____

# Journal

# Morning Practice

What is one thing that you are grateful for right now, something that brings you great joy?

_____

_____

_____

_____

Write out the question you drew from the deck.

_____

_____

_____

Is there one action you are willing to take today that moves you toward your question's answer?

_____

_____

_____

Do a short meditation of 1-2 minutes, just focusing on what's possible, focusing on your question.

Try not to over think it. Throughout your day let the universe do its job.

# Evening Practice

What is one thing you did that brought you joy today?

_____

_____

_____

_____

What one thing did you do today that you would like to do better.

_____

_____

_____

_____

One thing you will commit to do tomorrow that brings joy.

_____

_____

_____

If any answers were discovered you can write them here and/or in the journal page that follows.
Include any coincidences or powerful experiences.

_____

_____

_____

_____

# Journal

# Morning Practice

What is one thing that you are grateful for right now, something that brings you great joy?

_____

_____

_____

_____

_____

Write out the question you drew from the deck.

_____

_____

_____

_____

Is there one action you are willing to take today that moves you toward your question's answer?

_____

_____

_____

_____

Do a short meditation of 1-2 minutes, just focusing on what's possible, focusing on your question.

Try not to over think it. Throughout your day let the universe do its job.

# Evening Practice

What is one thing you did that brought you joy today?

_____

_____

_____

What one thing did you do today that you would like to do better.

_____

_____

_____

One thing you will commit to do tomorrow that brings joy.

_____

_____

_____

If any answers were discovered you can write them here and/or in the journal page that follows.
Include any coincidences or powerful experiences.

_____

_____

_____

# Journal

# Morning Practice

What is one thing that you are grateful for right now, something that brings you great joy?

Write out the question you drew from the deck.

Is there one action you are willing to take today that moves you toward your question's answer?

Do a short meditation of 1-2 minutes, just focusing on what's possible, focusing on your question.

Try not to over think it. Throughout your day let the universe do its job.

# Evening Practice

What is one thing you did that brought you joy today?

_____

_____

_____

What one thing did you do today that you would like to do better.

_____

_____

_____

One thing you will commit to do tomorrow that brings joy.

_____

_____

_____

If any answers were discovered you can write them here and/or in the journal page that follows.

Include any coincidences or powerful experiences.

_____

_____

_____

# Journal

# Morning Practice

What is one thing that you are grateful for right now, something that brings you great joy?

_____

_____

_____

_____

_____

Write out the question you drew from the deck.

_____

_____

_____

Is there one action you are willing to take today that moves you toward your question's answer?

_____

_____

_____

Do a short meditation of 1-2 minutes, just focusing on what's possible, focusing on your question.

Try not to over think it. Throughout your day let the universe do its job.

# Evening Practice

What is one thing you did that brought you joy today?

_____

_____

_____

What one thing did you do today that you would like to do better.

_____

_____

_____

One thing you will commit to do tomorrow that brings joy.

_____

_____

_____

If any answers were discovered you can write them here and/or in the journal page that follows.
Include any coincidences or powerful experiences.

_____

_____

_____

# Journal

Made in the USA
San Bernardino, CA
12 January 2020